THE
Irresistible
Church SERIES

Shout for JOY!

Engaging the **WHOLE CHURCH** in **ACCESSIBLE WORSHIP**

by Karen Roberts

 THE **IRRESISTIBLE CHURCH** SERIES

Joni and Friends

Shout for Joy!
Print Edition ISBN 978-1-946237-05-7
Kindle Edition ISBN 978-1-946237-06-4
ePUB Edition ISBN 978-1-946237-07-1

Author – Karen Roberts
Contributing Authors – Vinnie Adams, Ryan Roberts
Collaborators – Rob Branchflower, Bella Cameron
Contributing Editors - Ali Howard and Mike Dobes
Editor in Chief—Marc Stein

Produced by The Denzel Agency (www.denzel.org)
Cover and Interior Design: Rob Williams

For information or to order additional print copies of this
and other resources contact:

Joni and Friends International Disability Center
P.O. Box 3333, Agoura Hills, California 91376-3333
Email: churchrelations@joniandfriends.org
Phone: 818-707-5664

Kindle version available at www.irresistiblechurch.org

CONTENTS

Shout for joy to the Lord, all the earth. Worship the Lord with gladness; come before him with joyful songs. Know that the Lord is God. It is he who made us, and we are his; we are his people, the sheep of his pasture.

PSALM 100:1-3 (NIV)

Worship: A Conversation Initiated by God

What an amazing thought that God, the Creator of the universe, invites each one of us to enter his presence through worship. Worship can be described as a conversation between the Good Shepherd and his people, the sheep of his pasture. We respond to his invitation with shouts of joy and glad hearts because we are invited into relationship with our Creator and with our fellow sheep. Sometimes worship is a very personal conversation between God and an individual; at other times worship is a conversation that takes place between God and a community gathered in worship.

Fellow Sheep

Six years ago, I met a young man named Paul at a Joni and Friends Family Retreat. Paul was born with physical limitations that made it difficult for him to breathe, and he spent much of his time in a wheel-chair. Paul loved to worship the Lord and lead others in worship. While Paul was unable to physically stand in worship, his mind and spirit rose as he lifted his voice to sing his favorite hymns and songs of praise.

During a time of worship Paul asked his buddy if she would be willing to kneel before the Lord on his behalf because he was unable to get out of his wheelchair to do so. What a powerful request! I learned a lot about worship from this young man. I am physically able to kneel before the Lord whenever I want, and yet I often do not.

Unfortunately, it is not hard for me to imagine a scenario in which that request never met my ears or strengthened my heart. There are many "Pauls" in the body of Christ, and yet many of them are unseen, unnoticed, or unwelcomed by the church. Few churches are equipped and prepared to welcome families affected by disability and accommodate their needs, even for an hour on Sunday. Few people feel prepared to walk together with them in a communal journey of faith and worship. And yet, despite the challenges associated with disability, my own faith story and that of our local Joni and

Friends office would have a gaping hole and would feel incomplete without Paul and those like him. To not know Paul would mean missing part of our story, part of the body of Christ, part of the kingdom of God here on Earth.

Do you long to be part of a church community that welcomes people like Paul? Do you long to be part of a church community where people of all abilities enter his presence, uniting their voices and hearts in praise and thanksgiving? A church community where the sounds of worship include a "wheelchair rolling down the aisle, the tap of a cane, and the sound of people with differing intellectual disabilities lifting their voices in praise and prayer"?[1] If so, we pray this book will help you and your whole church engage in worship that is accessible and welcoming to all of God's children.

If you are a pastor, a worship leader, a musician, a parent of a child with special needs, a person with a disability: be encouraged. God is at work in his Church. More and more churches are becoming *Irresistible*: authentic communities built on the hope of Christ that compel people affected by disability to fully belong. To fully belong includes entering God's presence as the community gathers in worship.

A Journey of Attitudes

Dan Vander Plaats, Director of Advancement of Elim Christian Services, often asks, "Have you ever noticed there are no asterisks in the Bible?" For example, he notes that there is no asterisk in Psalm 100:3. The psalmist did not write, " . . . we are his people,* and the sheep of his pasture . . . " *(except people with disabilities). God's invitation to worship extends to people of all abilities. A church that is seeking to experience accessible worship embraces the truth of Ephesians 2:10: "For we are his workmanship, created in Christ Jesus for good works, which God prepared beforehand, that we should walk in them." Seeing each person as God sees them often requires individuals and faith communities to go on a journey of attitudes. We begin by seeing each individual as someone created in God's image (see Genesis 1:26-28), fearfully and wonderfully made (see Psalm 139:14). I love how Dan Vander Plaats describes this journey in *5 Stages: Changing Attitudes.*📖

📖 This symbol indicates that there are supplemental resources that correspond with this topic at http://www.joniandfriends.org/church-relations/

The 5 Stages:
1. Ignorance
2. Pity
3. Care
4. Friendship
5. Co-laborers

In this journey an individual or a church begins at stage 1: ignorance. In this stage an individual or church has no relationship or desire to be in a relationship with a person affected by disability. From there this individual or church would move to stage 2: pity. In this stage an individual or church see people in their community impacted by disability, but their response may be to feel sorry for them or even look down on them. Sadly, this is often our natural response.

If an individual or a church is willing, the journey continues to stage 3: care. This stage might be described as "ministry to" people impacted by disabilities. God calls us to continue the journey to stage 4: friendship. In this stage, we begin to build relationships that impact us when we come together in worship. There is mutuality and a sense of belonging that happen as we relate to one another. Finally, stage 5 is co-laborer, where people of all abilities use their gifts in ministry and service together.

As a parallel, we see Jesus, who looked on the crowds with compassion, cared for the broken, initiated relationship with them, and sent them out as his disciples. He still does this today and calls us to do the same.

When a church embarks on this journey, worship becomes accessible as people of differing abilities respond to God, greet one another, lift praises, hear the Word, share communion, pray for one another, and send each other out to serve a hurting world as co-laborers.

Journey of One Church

In my church, there are large stained-glass windows made of many broken pieces of glass, all shapes and sizes, put together by an artist to visually share the gospel story. One Sunday our pastor asked us to consider how we are all designed by the master Creator, and to recognize that, like the pieces of glass, we are all broken and in need of his saving grace. God began to open our eyes and show us that some of our pieces were missing. Our church began a journey of changing attitudes as we realized that without people impacted by disability our church family was not complete.

In response to this realization, a small group from our church began serving lunches at a day center for adults with disabilities. The first time we served lunch, the group was very friendly and greeted each person, but we mostly stayed behind the serving tables (stage 1: ignorance). A few people in our group expressed that they felt sorry for some of the individuals we met (stage 2: pity). But, we kept coming (stage 3: care), and God began changing our attitudes so that now we don't stay behind the serving tables; instead, everyone is talking and sharing a meal together (stage 4: friendship). Several adults from the day center now attend our monthly Friendship Bible Club and use their musical gifts as part of the club's worship band (stage 5: co-laborers).

Accessible Worship:
The Actions of All People

Robert E. Webber stated, "Worship is a verb."[2] So, how can we plan worship that will allow people of all abilities to be actively engaged? How can we communicate that each person has a role to play in the conversation between God and his people? Our worship often involves physical actions like lifting our voices and hands in praise, taking communion, bringing our offering, being baptized, and extending greetings to others. These physical actions are right, proper, and beautiful; but more important are the posture and attitude of our hearts, as my friend Paul reminded us.

While my friend Paul was physically unable to kneel before the Lord, the posture of his heart was one of humility and praise. Paul knew he had a part to play in the body of Christ by helping lead others in worship before the Lord.

Last year, I joined Paul's family and hundreds of friends in a memorial service for Paul. The number and diversity of people gathered on that day was an amazing testimony of God's grace displayed in Paul's life. During the service, the chaplain spoke about a conversation she had with Paul a few days before the Lord called him home. When she asked Paul what he was looking forward to in heaven, he replied, "I am looking forward to kneeling before the throne." Regardless of Paul's abilities or disabilities, he worshiped in such a way that he influenced and encouraged everyone around him—what a beautiful example!

Worship that is accessible to people of all abilities creates opportunities for individuals to respond to God in a variety of multi-sensory ways, including sights, sounds, and even smells. Worship that is accessible encourages participation from everyone. In accessible worship, we engage with God and with one another.

So, how do we begin?

Hospitality:
Accessibility and Acceptance

I love the words of Romans 15:7: "Therefore welcome one another as Christ has welcomed you, for the glory of God." Churches that desire to have accessible worship should be welcoming, showing equal concern for each person and affirming their importance in Christ. In much the same way that you clean your home and cook a meal in preparation for visiting guests, it is important to make intentional preparations as your church strives toward accessible worship so that each person feels valued and welcomed. The first book in the *Irresistible Church* series, *Start with Hello*, discusses the significance of both accessibility and acceptance. As you prepare to engage in accessible worship, you will want to consider the layout of your facilities and spend time getting to know the individuals affected by disability within your congregation.

Accessibility

There are many excellent resources available to help congregations make their entire facility accessible. 📚 But right now, let's take a look at the sanctuary, or worship area, of your church.

Seating: Is there accessible seating available in your worship space, preferably scattered throughout rather than clustered together? In my church, the young adults like to sit together right up front in the center section. We recently remodeled to include accessible seating in several places, but there was no accessible seating available in the "young adults" area. Richard, a young man and wheelchair user, wanted to sit with his friends. Happily, the decision was made to create an accessible space in that section, allowing Richard to worship alongside his peers.

Stage: Is the platform area or stage accessible? This can be a challenge, even for churches that have accessible seating. But when churches make their stage accessible, it communicates a powerful message that people of all abilities can participate in and lead worship.

Visuals: If projection of visuals is used, can they be seen by persons standing in spirit (who use a wheelchair) when others are standing in body? It is also important to consider how to create visuals that are accessible to people with visual impairments. Check out the online appendices for this book to see some specific suggestions. ☙

Audio Aids: Does your church provide sign language interpretation in your worship services? Does your church provide other audio aids? With recent advances in technology, there are many options to explore, including real-time translation services, audio streaming, and hearing assistive systems that connect to smartphones or tablets. ☙

Training: Accessibility starts in the parking lot. It can be a great idea to provide disability etiquette training for parking lot attendants, ushers, and greeters. ☙ Individuals in these roles are often the first to welcome a new person to your church. They should be able to share with a visiting special needs family information about what is offered at your church. This might include accessible seating, audio aids, large-print or worship programs in Braille, and special needs ministry activities like small groups or children's worship. They should also be able to direct people to accessible bathroom facilities.

Sensory Accommodations: Some individuals with disabilities can be overwhelmed by sights and sounds. Providing a space where the music and sermon can be heard more quietly with less distraction can be a great idea if your facilities can accommodate such arrangements. If you do not have space for something like that, consider providing sound-limiting headphones to individuals with sensory sensitivity or providing small sensory items.

These considerations remind us how important it is to know our congregations and to provide choices that allow each person to engage in worship.

Acceptance

While it is important to make your facilities accessible, cultivating a culture of acceptance and love is of even more importance. If you are introducing your church to disability ministry for the first time, it can be a great idea to hold a Disability Awareness Sunday. This is a special time dedicated to educating and encouraging the people in your church to understand and embrace disability ministry. A Disability Awareness Sunday is a great opportunity to cast the vision of what it means for a church to become irresistible! 📚

Virtual Tours: Taking time to let families affected by disability know what it will be like to join your community in worship can be a great way for your ministry leaders to play a role in hospitality. Many churches post a virtual tour on their website, through video or pictures, to show prospective visitors their facilities and worship service.

Off-hours Tour: Arranging for a family to visit the worship space at a time when no one is around is another step of hospitality that helps special needs families feel more comfortable engaging in worship. Allowing an unfamiliar place to become familiar without a noisy crowd can make the process of getting acquainted with your church less overwhelming.

Planning Ahead: Knowing the order of each day's events can be very important to individuals affected by disability, particularly our friends on the autism spectrum. Worship leaders could make the order of worship and song lyrics available ahead of time to individuals and families impacted by disabilities. This extra step will go a long way in saying, "Welcome, we are glad you are part of our family!"

If it is our desire to have each person within our church community engaged in worship, then a good place to begin is by getting to know each other and creating an environment in which our friends affected by disability feel comfortable and welcomed. After considering the accessibility of your facilities and hearts, I encourage you to dig into the specifics of making your worship service accessible.

Notes
  1. Doug Mazza, President of Joni and Friends International Disability Ministry, Leadership Conference, 2014.
  2. Robert E. Webber, *Worship Is a Verb (Peabody, MA: Hendrickson Publishing, 2004), p. vii.*

Planning Accessible Worship

Gathering, Word, Response, Sending

Throughout centuries of Christian worship, there have been many different musical styles and traditions. Within each of the wonderful and varied expressions of worship is a common, biblical pattern of revelation and response woven into the various components. God reveals himself, and his people we respond in obedience, praise and service. We *gather* as God's people, coming together in corporate worship because he invites us to do so. In worship, God speaks to our hearts through his *Word*, and we *respond* in prayer, thanksgiving, communion and baptism. As corporate worship concludes, we *send* each other out with blessings and encouragement to serve the Lord throughout the week. We encourage one another to grow in relationship with our Savior, to live our lives as an act of worship. "I appeal to you therefore, brothers, by the mercies of God, to present your bodies as a living sacrifice, holy and acceptable to God, which is your spiritual worship" (Romans 12:1).

These four elements of worship (gathering, Word, response, sending) are known in some traditions as the fourfold pattern of worship. Some congregations follow this pattern exactly, while others use them as a general foundation for their worship service. Within the context of this book, we will use them as a roadmap, or guide, to planning accessible worship based on biblical principles. As you read through this next section, I encourage you to ask yourself, "How can I plan worship that will engage the whole congregation in accessible worship?"

Visuals can help us understand and remember, so I have included arrows to depict the movement of revelation and response that happens in each component of the fourfold pattern. The arrow pointing to the right indicates the movement that occurs when the body of believers gathers to worship. The arrow pointing down depicts the revelation that moves from God to man through God's written Word. The arrow pointing up reflects our response to God as seen through various components of worship. And the arrow pointing to the left indicates the movement of believers as we leave the church and influence our communities.

Gathering ▶

We are always in the presence of God, but when we gather together in intentional worship around his throne, we can have confidence that Jesus is in our midst. "Where two or three come together in my name, there am I with them" (Matthew 18:20). As we engage in corporate worship, we move from our individual lives and join with others.

There are many possible elements or acts of worship that can be included in the gathering, depending on your tradition or style of worship. The gathering, or opening, of your church service might include words of welcome or a greeting, a call to worship or an opening prayer, expressions of praise, confession, and assurance of forgiveness.

Whether your style of worship is traditional, contemporary, convergent, or a blend of several styles, these various elements seek to gather the people of God together and prepare us to hear the preaching of the Word.

Practical Ideas for Making the Gathering Accessible

You might be thinking, *This is all great in theory, but how do we actually make these elements of worship more accessible?* Below are a few practical ideas on how to make the gathering portion of your service accessible.

Words of Welcome: To encourage participation, consider using a consistent phrase, such as "God is good...all the time!... All the time...God is good!" Call-and-response greetings add to the feeling that everyone is involved in worship.

Call to Worship: Using short, repeated phrases, such as "His love endures forever," throughout your call to worship helps engage the entire congregation. You could also create a slideshow or video depicting people of various ages and abilities sharing Scripture.

Opening Prayer: In many churches, the opening prayer or invocation is offered by the pastor. However, in some churches this prayer might be offered by the worship leader or lay people. Depending on your worship practice, you could consider inviting one or more individuals affected by disability to share an opening prayer.

Expressions of Praise: What if instead of saying, "Please stand," the pastor or worship leader said, "Please rise in body or in spirit" or "Please stand as you are able" when inviting the congregation to stand as they offer expressions of praise? Or perhaps they could say, "Let's lift our hearts, hands, or voices in worship." Such changes are small but significant ways to communicate to those with disabilities, "You are welcome here!"

Confession and Assurance of Forgiveness: It is not our abilities, culture, age, or ethnicity that prohibit us from entering into conversation with our Creator. Rather, it is our sin. Therefore, because Christ's atonement is great enough to cover all our sin, then anyone who confesses ". . . that Jesus Christ is Lord, to the glory of God the Father" (Philippians 2:11) is welcome to the conversation—regardless of abilities or disabilities!

Some churches include a time of confession as part of their weekly corporate worship service. This time may include a song, a prayer of confession, or a time of silence during which individuals can make their hearts right before the Lord. Throughout the worship service we see a rhythm of revelation and response. In confession, we humble our hearts and come before God to say, "I'm sorry." If you desire to include this element in your worship service, consider making it more accessible by using short, repeated phrases that can be sung or spoken, such as "Forgive us" or "Lord, have mercy." If your church has a practice of inviting people to come to the cross during this time, make sure that the area is accessible to all. You can encourage people to bow or kneel in body *or in spirit* before the Lord as a nonverbal way to say, "I'm sorry." Your pastor or worship leader might even teach the church body some sign language by making a fist (representing the letter *S* in sign language) and moving your fist in a circle over your chest to say, "I'm sorry." As you incorporate opportunities for both personal and corporate confession of sin, it can be followed with a time of praise and gratitude for God's gracious forgiveness. Allow me to share with you an example of an accessible Prayer of Confession written by Vinnie Adams, Worship Leader and Special Needs Ministry Director of Faith Church in Dyer, Indiana.

As the readers say, "Sorry," all worshipers can use their fist to sign the letter *S*, moving it in a circle as described above. It is a great idea to include readers of differing abilities.

Reader 1: God, you are an awesome God! We thank you for loving us and accepting us into your family, just as we are, because of Jesus. We admit and confess to you today that we aren't always very good at loving you back. In fact, we mess up a lot; so we take this moment to confess these things to you and say, "We're sorry." And we do it, Lord, knowing that you forgive us and still have an amazing love for us—for which we say, "Thank you."

Reader 2: For the times when we say bad words and think bad thoughts, we say, "Sorry."

Reader 1: For the times when we forget to rest and remember that you are God, we say, "Sorry."

Reader 2: For the times when we don't obey our moms and dads, or don't love our family members, we say, "Sorry."

Reader 1: For the times when we are mean to others, whether they are nice to us or not, we say, "Sorry."

Reader 2: For the times when we are jealous of others or try to take things that aren't ours, we say, "Sorry."

Reader 1: For the times we don't listen to you and want to do our own thing, we say, "Sorry."

Reader 1: Thank you for forgiving us over and over again.

Reader 2: God, we need your help.

Reader 1: Would you fill us with your Holy Spirit to help us every moment of every day? We desire to live for you and love you well.

Reader 2: We ask this in Jesus' name, amen.

Intentionally including people of all abilities in the gathering of your church service will set the tone for the remainder of your time together in worship. Let's continue considering how we can create an inclusive worship environment as we look at the preaching of the Word.

Word ▼

God revealing himself through Scripture is a core component of worship. First Timothy 4:13 says, "Until I come, devote yourself to the public reading of Scripture, to exhortation, to teaching." Through the Word, God's story of creation, man's fall, redemption, and re-creation is proclaimed. At the center of this story is Christ, our risen Lord, who is present with the community gathered in worship.

During the worship service, God speaks to his people through the Word. While this portion of the service is typically centered around a sermon or a message, it might also include Scripture readings, music, and testimonies.

Practical Ideas for Making the Word Accessible

As it is our goal to present the gospel in a way that people of all abilities can understand, it is worth pausing to consider how this might be accomplished. The following are a few suggestions to consider:

Scripture Reading: As appropriate in your context, consider using a simpler version of the Bible, such as the *International Children's Bible*, *The Message*, or the *New International Reader's Version*. You might invite readers of differing abilities or individuals using communication devices to read, sign, or otherwise communicate a passage of Scripture. You could also create a video with people of varying abilities reciting Scripture and then present it during the worship service.

Sermon or Message: People of all ages and abilities process information in a variety of ways. You may have heard someone say that they are a visual learner, experiential learner, auditory learner, or that they learn best some other way. A Chinese proverb says, "Tell me, I forget. Show me, I remember. Involve me, I understand." When Scripture is preached in ways that show us and involve us, we generally remember and understand more easily. Consider incorporating visuals, dance, digital media, drama, and storytelling as ways to present God's Word. Keep in mind that abstract language may need more explanation to be understood. Often, our friends with special needs understand better when difficult ideas are explained with straightforward, literal language.

Jesus was the master storyteller. Listeners were drawn to his simple language and vivid word pictures, like the story of the Prodigal Son or the Good Samaritan. We tend to remember stories more than facts; stories are something to which we can relate in our own lives. When Jesus told a story, he typically had one main point that was easy to understand. He used familiar vocabulary and descriptive language that allowed his listeners to picture the scene. His stories were relevant, engaging, and filled with truth. Stories are powerful and accessible.

As you incorporate the Word into worship, don't be afraid to try new things! Ask members of your congregation who are affected by disability how they learn best, and consider integrating those learning styles. Simply by asking and taking the time to think about how you present the truths of Scripture you are creating an inclusive and accessible environment.

Messages on Suffering: People living with disability have much to teach the church about what it means to believe in, rely on, and cling to the hope found in Jesus Christ. Sermons or messages that focus on various themes of suffering and God's faithfulness will encourage and speak to all hearts. Your pastor or teacher can teach the congregation through the Word to see Christ as the suffering servant, present with them as they gather in worship.

For example, in the book of Daniel we find the story of Shadrach, Meshach and Abednego, who were thrown into a fiery furnace because of their faith in God. As King Nebuchadnezzar threatened them with death, they said, "...our God whom we serve is able to deliver us from the burning fiery furnace, and he will deliver us out of your hand, O king. But if not, be it known to you, O king, that we will not serve your gods or worship the golden image that you have set up" (Daniel 3:16-18). A message preached on these brave young men and their steadfast faith in the face of suffering could bring encouragement to parents of a special needs child who has just received a life-altering diagnosis. They may ask, "Do we believe that God can heal our child? Do we have enough faith?" If God does not bring physical healing, they may struggle, asking, "Do we need more faith?"

It is natural for us to ask God why in the midst of suffering. However, our worship services do not always allow space or ways for people to ask God this question. Many pastors and worship leaders feel this tension, but they may not know how to address it. Incorporating Psalms, expressions of lament or grief, and even silence is a practice that can help address this question as you strive to make the conversation of worship accessible. The Psalms and other Scriptures that remind us of the hope of Christ amid everyday circumstances and struggles are encouraging to all, including individuals and families impacted by disability. The *Beyond Suffering Bible*, a copy of the *New Living Translation* that has been paired with devotions and encouraging insights from Joni Eareckson Tada, is a great resource to reference when studying these Scriptures.

At a recent Inclusive Worship Symposium, I participated in a workshop on worship and suffering. The participants shared stories about when they had questioned God. Individuals from this workshop then prayed expressions of lament during the concluding worship of the conference: "Be with my family. I miss my dad." "I lost my grandma and my roommate." "Dear heavenly Father, bless the hard times I am having right now and give me peace." In between these verbal expressions, worshipers sang a short, repeated musical phrase from a Chris Tomlin song: "Lord, have mercy, Christ have mercy, Lord, have mercy on me." Combining expressions of grief with worship allows us to express the turmoil in our hearts while still embracing an attitude of thanksgiving toward God.

Testimonies: As God's story of redemption is proclaimed, we begin to see our place in that story as his redeemed people. His story transforms ours. Inviting someone to share how his story has influenced theirs is a powerful way to make the Word of God accessible. You might do this by including a time of testimony from someone in your congregation that illustrates the truth being taught in the message. For example, if the message was based on 2 Corinthians 12:9, "My grace is sufficient for you, for my power is made perfect in weakness," then a person with a disability can share her story of how God has strengthened her and moved in her life. This can be a compelling moment in worship. Testimonies transfer the truth of the gospel into the reality of our everyday lives.

As we come to a greater understanding of Christ and the gospel through the Word, our hearts naturally overflow in worship. We have looked at planning accessible worship beginning with the *gathering* and proclamation of the *Word*, but we can't stop there. Let's continue to discover how worship can be made accessible to people of all abilities by discussing our *response* in the next section.

Response ▲

At the very heart of worship is gratitude. The conversation between God and his people often includes a time of thanksgiving. Worship that is engaging to all will offer a variety of ways for people of all ages and abilities to express gratitude to God.

The rhythm of revelation and response between God and his people continues as we respond to the Word. Our worshipful response to God's truth can take many different forms, but several that commonly occur in church services today include communion or Eucharist, baptism, receiving the offering, and praise and worship.

Responding Through Communion: The understanding and observance of the Lord's Supper—also called the Table, communion, or Eucharist—can vary between each tradition, denomination, or church community. But what is common to all is the truth that communion binds the body of Christ together. Mark Stephenson, a disability ministry leader, once said, "As many grains are gathered into one loaf, partaking of the elements binds God's people together into one. Ironically, when church leaders ignore the unique needs of worshipers with disabilities, some are excluded from the sacrament whose very name includes the word union."[1] Mark encourages churches to model inclusion not only by inviting people with disabilities to partake of communion, but also by inviting them to participate in serving communion, helping to pass the plate, or holding the bread when worshipers come forward to receive it.

Intentionality and planning are one way to show love. Think through how you can show concern and affirm one another's equal importance in Christ as you plan for the observance of communion. For example, you can provide the option of gluten-free wafers for those with dietary restrictions, or offer to help handle the elements for those with physical limitations. If the tradition at your church is for people to come forward to receive the elements, you might invite the elderly and wheelchair users to remain in their seats and serve them there. It is also a good idea to plan home visits so that individuals who are homebound can receive communion.

Like creating a virtual tour to welcome a new family, you could create a "Communion Story" video that outlines the various components of how your church observes communion. You might even find that offering a time for an individual to practice communion outside of a worship service is a helpful step.

Find out if your denomination has resources to assist individuals with disabilities to prepare for and participate in communion. For example, in churches that require that individuals be baptized prior to taking communion, explore the steps you might take so that people of all abilities who believe in Christ can be baptized and partake in communion. There are several excellent resources included in the online appendices to further explore this topic. 📖

Responding Through Baptism: Regardless of how your church embraces the practice of baptism, it is important that people with disabilities are offered the opportunity to be baptized. As with communion, there are ways that churches can help individuals with disabilities prepare for and participate in baptism.

Many churches have a process, or steps, that individuals must take to prepare for baptism. Usually these steps address the beliefs of the heart and the physical action of the baptism. Churches striving to be accessible need to address both components.

For example, if a church requires an individual to attend a class or follow a curriculum in preparation for baptism, they might make adaptations in the training material to make it more easily understood. 📖 Or, instead of attending the class, perhaps an elder or pastor of the church could meet one on one with individuals affected by disability to help them understand the significance of baptism and determine if there is a solid understanding and desire before moving forward. For churches that believe baptism should be expressed through immersion, they may need to consider what accommodations are possible for an individual who desires to be baptized but is unable to be immersed because of their disability.

Allow me to share with you a story about B.J., an outgoing young man with Down syndrome and apraxia, a disability that restricts his ability to speak. He has been highly involved in the church throughout his life and is now a regular member of the young adult class.

B.J. often serves as a greeter at his church, and part of his responsibility is to hand a bulletin to worshipers as they enter the sanctuary. One Sunday morning, B.J. read on the front of the bulletin that a baptism service was scheduled for the following month and that anyone wanting to be baptized should let the church office know. He was very excited and told his mom he wanted to be baptized! At the end of the service, he hurried to set up a time to meet with his pastor.

In preparation to meet with the pastor B.J.'s parents reviewed the significance of baptism with him, trying not to put words in his mouth. They wanted all of B.J.'s answers to come from his heart. When the pastor asked, "What does Jesus mean to you?" B.J. answered, "Jesus died for my sins and he rose again." Then his pastor asked, "Why do you want to be baptized?" B.J. responded, saying, "I want to obey Jesus and follow him. I want everyone to know I love Jesus." Smiling, the pastor said he thought B.J. was ready to be baptized.

The pastor and B.J.'s parents discussed how it might work best to facilitate B.J.'s baptism, considering his special needs. Although the pastor could understand B.J.'s communication during their one-on-one conversation, it would be difficult for B.J. to express himself to the congregation in a worship service. They decided to program B.J.'s responses into his iPhone so that on the morning of his baptism the pastor could ask the rehearsed questions and put the microphone next to B.J.'s phone, allowing the congregation to hear his pre-recorded responses.

B.J.'s mom captured the heart behind this book perfectly when she said, "Cognitively challenged young people are capable of comprehending much more than we imagine possible. They love to worship!"

Responding Through Offering: Another aspect of responding involves the giving of tithes and offerings. While many different traditions and styles exist, the financial response of worship and "giving back" to God is an important part of following Christ. In a similar sensibility as communion, we must consider how to make sharing an offering accessible. If a plate or bucket is being passed, encourage your ushers to think about how they can assist people affected by disability, especially individuals with limited or no movement of hands or arms. Some churches choose to collect an offering at the front of the sanctuary during worship; others collect it through containers at the back of the church without designating a specific time to do so. Regardless of your setup, the key is to consider how you can make this style of worship available to individuals affected by disability. As you strive to do so, you might want to consider the following questions: Is it possible to provide assistance for individuals at their seats, or have an usher or other volunteer available to assist as necessary during this time? Are the offering containers set at a height that remains accessible for individuals in a wheelchair? Could your current practices hinder an individual from giving cheerfully, and could this dilemma be easily remedied through usher assistance, clearer prompts of the process, or maybe a complete change of how offering is received? As with all other aspects of accessibility, intentionality and planning provide the greatest opportunity for churches to provide space for individuals affected by disability to fully belong. Perhaps the best place to start is simply by asking church members who are affected by disability what obstacles might exist and the solutions they recommend.

Responding Through Serving and Leading: A very capable young woman with cerebral palsy recently shared with me that the greatest need of individuals with disabilities is to be needed. As your church works to develop habits and practices that allow worship to be accessible, please remember to find ways in which people of all abilities can serve in the various ministries of your church.

There are two churches in Illinois that provide beautiful examples of opening the door for individuals with disabilities to lead and serve through praise and worship. College Church in Wheaton, Illinois, has several musical groups that welcome members of all abilities and include singing, playing chimes, percussion instruments, and drama. These groups share the gospel through performances in College Church's worship services as well as through other concerts around the world. The Praetorium Sign Language Church and Community Choir is part of the Stone Temple Church of Chicago. This is a choir of individuals with hearing impairments who use their musical skills and expressive sign language to lead others in a unique and accessible style of worship. I recently attended a chapel service at Moody Bible Institute where members of the Praetorium Sign Language Choir were joined by Moody students learning American Sign Language (ASL). It was a beautiful picture of all abilities leading together in worship.

Most churches have special services and musical performances for holidays like Thanksgiving, Christmas, Lent, or Easter. Consider how you could invite people of all abilities to participate in these events.

There are many other areas within your church and worship service where people with varying abilities can serve. A few ideas might include running PowerPoint slides, helping with multi-media and graphics, working as ushers and greeters, or joining the prayer team. If your church has any sort of drama team, this can also be a great opportunity for children, teens, and adults with disabilities to worship the Lord through their participation.

As you work to integrate people of varying abilities into the components of your worship service, remember to begin by getting to know each individual: their strengths, interests, and passions.

God desires for *all* his people to worship him. By including our friends with disabilities in the worship service and encouraging them to participate in the response, we are bringing him glory and edifying the body of Christ.

The Sending ◀

As the worship service concludes, we should ask ourselves the question, "What happens next?" As believers leave the service and return to their own lives, there is a reversal of the movement of the gathering. Although the corporate worship service has ended, we encourage one another to go forth, to love those around us, and to serve the Lord. Worship begins with an invitation from God to enter his presence, and it becomes a lifestyle as the Lord sends us out into the world to live our lives as a spiritual act of worship. The apostle Paul wrote, "I appeal to you therefore, brothers, by the mercies of God, to present your bodies as a living sacrifice, holy and acceptable to God, which is your spiritual worship" (Romans 12:1). We worship God simply by how we live our daily lives. Each week we can attend a worship service at church and glorify God together. But as we leave those services with a blessing, God sends us out into our communities to be a blessing so that others might know his love and mercy.

At my church, we end each service by singing "My Friends, May You Grow in Grace." When we sing the last line, we join hands, stretching across the aisle to make sure every person has a hand to hold. One day, Jenny, a woman with an intellectual disability, noticed that a man two rows in front of her was standing alone. Jenny left her seat, approached the man, and offered her hand as they sang the last part of the song together. Seeing this brought a tear to my eye and a smile to my face, what a beautiful picture of the body of Christ!

Coming together to worship the Lord corporately is important, but equally important is how we worship the Lord in our individual daily lives. Regardless of age, ability, or background, we are all designed to bring glory to God. As your church becomes more irresistible, you may want to consider how you can partner with individuals and families affected by disability throughout the week. Remember the five stages of changing attitudes that we looked at earlier? The last stage is "co-laborer," where people of all abilities serve together. Our friends affected by disability have many gifts and talents they can use to be a testimony of God's goodness throughout the week.

Thus far, we have considered practical strategies to engage your whole church in accessible worship using the fourfold pattern of gathering, Word, response, and sending as a framework. As we continue our conversation, let's look at some specific strategies to engage children and youth affected by disability in accessible worship.

Note

1. Taken from "Inclusive Communion" by Mark Stephenson from *Reformed Worship*. Reprinted with permission © Faith Alive Christian resources.

Accessible Worship
for Children/Youth

Just as churches have varied traditions and styles of worship, churches also vary in their approach to worship for different age groups. Some churches choose to have all ages participate together in corporate worship; some choose to have a separate time of worship for children and youth. Other churches have a combination of these two practices. Whatever format your church uses, here are some practical ideas to engage children and youth in accessible worship.

Multi-sensory: Many children and youth are visual learners. Adding pictures or objects to help teach songs or lessons is an effective way to engage children and youth of all abilities. For example, you might give each worshiper a pipe cleaner and demonstrate how to bend it into the shape of a heart. As the group sings a worship song, they can raise their pipe-cleaner hearts up to the Lord during the chorus.

Involving children and youth in creating visuals for the worship environment is another tool to help them engage in an accessible conversation with God.

For example, a small group could work together to create a large "stained-glass window" simply by each person dipping their fingers in window paint and adding their fingerprints on sections of a window-pane. Another group might create banners for the worship environment to use as a processional during a song of praise.

Adding motions to a song is a fun way to encourage children or youth in worship. Ask individuals who use ASL to help others learn the signs to a song or a Scripture passage. You might even explore the possibility of having the children or youth lead the congregation in corporate worship or include a youth-led worship song as part of an outreach event.

You can also encourage the writing and sharing of original songs. This could be done in a group setting or individually. This is a wonderful way for an individual to have a conversation with God that can be shared with others in a worship context.

Addressing Difficult Questions: Children and youth with disabilities often ask questions like the following: "Does Jesus know when I'm hurting?" "If Jesus loves me, why doesn't he fix my disability?" "Is Jesus disappointed in me when I'm not brave?" "Does Jesus know when I'm going to die?"[1] Including Scripture and biblical stories into times of worship that speak to God's love and sovereignty can help answer these questions and encourage children of all abilities in their spiritual walk with the Lord. It is also a way to bring the rhythm of revelation and response into times of worship for children and teens. It is a dialogue of asking questions and finding the answers as God reveals himself through Scripture.

Sometimes we can underestimate the power of the Holy Spirit to engage children and youth of varying abilities in worship. We may limit what we present or offer to young people because we are unsure of how it will be understood or received, but there is a powerful Spirit-to-spirit connection that happens beyond our limited understanding. Every now and then we catch a glimpse of the Spirit at work, and we are in awe. Take for example a group of five elementary-aged children who attended a Joni and Friends' Family Retreat. One afternoon this group of children arrived for a time of worship, but there was one complication: all five were severely and profoundly impaired. They could not verbally participate. What to do?

The leader quickly asked the Lord for wisdom and then knelt before one of the children. She touched the child's knee gently, called him by name, and asked, "Do you know that Jesus loves you?" Immediately his head shot up, he made direct eye contact, and his face became wreathed in a huge smile! In shock, the leader moved to the next child and did the same thing with the same reaction. As the leader approached each child and asked this question, each of the five children responded in the same way! With all five pairs of eyes fixed on her face, the leader began to sing, "Jesus loves me, this I know." Five heads bobbed with the song as their smiles grew bigger and brighter, reaching all the way to their eyes. The atmosphere was electric! When the song ended and the worship time concluded, the light went out of their eyes, their smiles faded, and their heads sank slowly back onto their chests as their buddies stood in shock. Finally, one buddy whispered, "We are standing on holy ground!" That day God made it clear that physical and intellectual disabilities are no hindrance to his Spirit connecting with the heart and soul of those with special needs!

Storytelling: As was true with corporate worship, an effective and accessible way of sharing the Word with children and youth is through storytelling. As you prepare a Sunday school lesson, you might want to ask yourself a few questions:

- Does the lesson tell a story with one main point that students can relate to their daily lives?
- Can listeners picture the scenes and understand the vocabulary used in this story?
- Will this story provide sensory experiences that facilitate understanding?
- Is this story fun to tell and engaging for listeners?
- How can I create concrete experiences to convey biblical concepts?

As an example, if you want to present the gospel to children and youth affected by disability, you could give each young person a simple, white paper heart along with brown, black and grey crayons. Encourage them to color their hearts as a reminder of how our sins make our hearts "dirty." You can then explain that we can't clean our hearts and make them white again—Jesus must do it for us. The children and youth can crumple up their "dirty hearts" and place them in a basket at the foot of a simple wooden cross. After leaving their hearts at the cross, they can pass through a "car wash" made from strips of blue plastic tablecloth hanging from a PVC frame. This will help them understand the cleansing work of Jesus. Finally, after having left behind their old, dirty hearts and being washed clean, each person can be given a small, stuffed white heart to remind them of the clean, soft hearts that Jesus gives us when we believe in him.

Worship Planning: Consider having a consistent format for times of worship. You can structure your worship service in many different ways. One example would be to use the structure of the fourfold pattern discussed earlier for corporate worship as a format for planning accessible worship for children and youth. Plan ways to welcome the group, bringing everyone's focus to a time of worship (*gather*). Following the welcome, present a teaching (*Word*), and then take time to explore together, "What does this mean to me?" (*response*). As the kids leave Sunday school, pray and encourage one another to make a difference in someone else's life throughout the week (*send*).

Repetition and consistent practices, such as using a common opening or sending song, could also be beneficial. Posting a visual schedule or providing individual schedules is another effective tool, allowing youth to follow along throughout the service.

Note
1. Joni Eareckson Tada & Steve Bundy with Pat Verbal, *Beyond Suffering: A Christian View on Disability Ministry* (Christian Institute on Disability, Joni and Friends International Disability Center, 2011), pp. 173-175.

Why Does It Matter?

We have considered many practical aspects of accessible worship, but I don't want to simply leave you with practical ideas. I want to leave you with an understanding of why this matters, of why accessible worship is so important. To do so, allow me to give you behind-the-scenes insight into why Vacation Bible School (VBS) at a Southern California church was so special last summer.

Each summer, churches across the country hold VBS to teach kids the gospel and get them excited about the Bible. For Rick* and his twin sister, Jenni, VBS came with mixed emotions. Jenni had been able to enjoy VBS for many years, but because Rick struggles with autism and is largely nonverbal, he had never been able to attend. Last summer, Calvary Community Church made it possible for both Jenni and Rick to attend by intentionally structuring the program to include children with special needs. Rick was able to participate with the assistance of a buddy, and Jenni participated by serving as a buddy for a child with special needs. They were beyond excited to finally attend together!

*Please note: Names in this story have been changed to protect their privacy.

Through the course of the week, 700 kids with varying levels of ability gathered together to learn about Jesus and worship him. At one point in the week, the videographer captured a truly beautiful moment: Rick was standing among his peers, passionately singing a song of praise with his hands lifted high in worship to his heavenly Father. He was clearly having the time of his life!

When a photo of this moment was shown to Rick's mother, she could not hold back her tears. She was deeply moved to see her son fully engaged in VBS for the first time and truly belonging in the church.

Why does accessible worship matter? It matters because people matter. It matters because the gospel matters. By structuring our churches in a way that allows *all people* to worship, we are communicating the truth that *all people* can have a life-giving relationship with Christ. There is nothing more important in this life than believing and sharing the gospel. By engaging in accessible worship, we are opening the door for *all people* to believe and share the gospel.

A Benediction

The truth that Christ is present in our worship is a blessing and a mystery beyond our understanding. The Holy Spirit connects with our spirit in a profound way that is not dependent upon our abilities but on the grace and love of our heavenly Father. Through Christ, he invites us to enter communion with him and community with one another. Together, people of all abilities enter the presence of God—a truly indescribable gift.

A Word to Individuals with Disabilities

Psalm 150:6 says, "Let everything that has breath praise the Lord! Praise the Lord!" God created us to worship. Worship is not dependent on our abilities but on the grace of Jesus Christ. While our bodies may suffer from disability, there are no disabled souls. We are all complete in Christ. In him all our brokenness is made whole.

Truthfully, the Church is not complete without people impacted by disabilities. We are the body of Christ, called by name to gather around God's throne as co-laborers and to minister together. I hope that in reading this book you are encouraged because God is at work in his church. Please pray that more individuals and families impacted by disability will fully belong to church communities gathered together in worship.

A Word to Parents and Caregivers

No one knows your child or loved one like you do. Please remember that we need your help and your grace as we learn how to best serve your loved ones. You can help your church leadership get to know your child. I encourage you to share with them which parts of the worship service will be the most engaging for your loved one and start there.

Emily Colson, a special needs mom, tells a story in her book *Dancing with Max* of when she and her son, Max, took steps for him to participate in worship after being absent from the church body for some time. The first time they went back to church, they began just by coming at the end of the service when everyone socialized. Emily cringed when she saw Max lift a chair over his head, but then relaxed as she saw a few men from the church directing Max to stack the chair with the others. As the crowd diminished, one of the men who had been stacking chairs approached Max and said, "Max, we could use you on the Grunt

Crew." The Grunt Crew is the team that handles the setup and tear-down for their church.

Speaking on that experience, Emily shared, "Someone told Max he was needed. That one sentence, that one invitation, opened the door for us. Max now serves as a greeter as well. That one simple invitation told Max, and me, that my son was needed."[1]

As you engage in the body of Christ, please remember that without you and your loved one, the body is not complete. We need you.

A Word to Special Needs Ministry Leaders

As special needs ministry grows, both within your church and in our communities, please keep looking for the most effective way to engage each child, youth, and adult with disabilities, drawing them into the worship life of your congregation. For some, that may be providing a worship buddy. For others, it might mean working with church leadership to provide a quiet area close to the worship space that allows individuals with sensory sensitivity to engage in worship without feeling overwhelmed. I also encourage you to continue working with other church staff members to bring disability awareness and education to the congregation—an ongoing need!

A Word to Pastors

Your role in casting the vision for your church is invaluable! As you introduce your congregants to the concept of accessible worship, you will set the tone. Your words of welcome from the platform can encourage your congregation along their journey of becoming an *irresistible church*. Remember Jenny, the young woman at my church with an intellectual disability who reached out to the man who was standing alone? One morning she spoke out loud during the message, something that is unusual at our church. Our pastor graciously did not see this as an interruption, but instead he spoke words of welcome and encouragement to her. In his response, our pastor modeled acceptance and belonging for the whole congregation.

This is a journey for the whole congregation. I believe it is a journey that God will lead and bless. If your church is just beginning this journey, I encourage you to check out the first book in the *Irresistible Church* series, *Start with Hello*.

A Word to Worship Leaders and Music Directors

If the concepts presented in this book are something that you would like to implement, but you don't know where to start, I encourage you to stop asking, "What do I need to add?" Instead, ask yourself, "What am I already doing that I could think about differently?"

As you embark on this journey toward accessible worship, one of the tensions you and your congregation may experience is the tension between excellence and inclusion. This is a tension that exists in many discussions as churches consider how people lead, engage, and participate in worship. How you choose to approach this tension will look unique for your church, but I ask you to have the conversation and lean into the tension. During this conversation, I encourage you to consider how your congregation is involved in your worship services and how lay people might be involved in planning the service. Look for ways that people with varying abilities can participate in and lead worship. As you actively collaborate to make worship accessible, remember to do so in concert with the leader of your special needs ministry and your church's pastoral leadership team.

Thinking about accessible worship may be new for many worship leaders, pastors and congregations. As you grow in this area, consider reading your favorite worship guides, blogs, and books with accessible worship in mind. Any philosophy or mode of worship can become more accessible. If you feel God is leading you to embrace the concepts presented in this book, please start with prayer, and start small. Choosing one idea to implement is a great way to get your feet wet and introduce your congregation to accessible worship. As you learn more about the families affected by disability in your congregation, you will have a better idea of how to make them feel included and welcomed.

A Word to All

Take a moment and look at the front cover of this book. Your eyes are drawn to the joyful expression of the young girl with visual impairment and the man playing the guitar. They are engaged in joyful, accessible worship. But did you notice the two girls watching in the background? There are many individuals and families "in the background." Let's become authentic communities and compel them to come in so that the Lord's house is full! Let's become irresistible so that "the sounds of worship in your church include a wheelchair rolling down the aisle, the tap of a cane and people with differing abilities lifting their voices and hearts together in praise and prayer."[2]

Note

1. Karen Roberts, personal interview, 10 May 2016.
2. Doug Mazza, 2014.

Becoming *Irresistible*

Luke 14 commands Christ followers to "Go quickly . . . find the blind, the lame, and the crippled . . . and compel them to come in!" While this sounds inspiring and daunting, exciting and overwhelming, motivating and frightening, all at the same time, what does it actually mean? How do we live and function within the church in such a way that families affected by disability are compelled to walk through our doors to experience the body of Christ?

We can certainly *compel* them by offering programs, ministries, events, and other church activities, but what if the compelling aspect was more about heart, culture, acceptance and embracing? What if our churches were overflowing with the hope of Jesus Christ . . . a hope not simply for those who "fit in" or look the part, but rather a hope to all, including the marginalized, downtrodden and outcast?

Becoming *Irresistible* is more than programs and activities—it is about a transformational work in our hearts . . . first as individuals and then as the body of Christ. *Irresistible* allows us to see each individual as he or she truly is: created in the image of God (Genesis 1:26-27), designed purposely as a masterpiece (Psalm 139:13-14), instilled with purpose, plans and dreams (Jeremiah 29:11), and a truly indispensable member of the kingdom of God (1 Corinthians 12:23). An *Irresistible Church* is an "authentic community built on the hope of Christ that compels people affected by disability to fully belong." It is powerful for a person to know that he or she is fully welcomed and belongs. *Irresistible* captures the heart of the church as it should be—how else do we explain the rapid growth and intense attraction to the church in the book of Acts? The heart of God was embodied through the people of God by the Spirit of God . . . and that is simply *Irresistible*!

The Irresistible Church Series is designed to help not only shape and transform the heart of the church, but also to provide the practical steps and activities to put *flesh* around the *heart* of the church—to help your church become a place for people to fully belong. Thank you for responding to the call to become *Irresistible*. It will not happen overnight, but it will happen. As with all good things, it requires patience and perseverance, determination and dedication, and ultimately an underlying trust in the faithfulness of God. May God bless you on this journey. Be assured that you are not alone—there are many on the path of *Irresistible*.

For more information or to join the community,
please visit www.irresistiblechurch.org.

Joni and Friends
INTERNATIONAL DISABILITY CENTER

Joni and Friends was established in 1979 by Joni Eareckson Tada, who at 17 was injured in a diving accident, leaving her a quadriplegic. Since its inception, Joni and Friends has been dedicated to extending the love and message of Christ to people who are affected by disability whether it is the disabled person, a family member, or friend. Our objective is to meet the physical, emotional, and spiritual needs of this group of people in practical ways.

Joni and Friends is committed to recruiting, training, and motivating new generations of people with disabilities to become leaders in their churches and communities. Today, the Joni and Friends International Disability Center serves as the administrative hub for an array of programs which provide outreach to thousands of families affected by disability around the globe. These include two radio programs, an award-winning television series, the Wheels for the World international wheelchair distribution ministry, Family Retreats which provide respite for those with disabilities and their families, Field Services to provide church training along with educational and inspirational resources at a local level, and the Christian Institute on Disability to establish a firm biblical worldview on disability-related issues.

From local neighborhoods to the far reaches of the world, Joni and Friends is striving to demonstrate to people affected by disability, in tangible ways, that God has not abandoned them—he is with them—providing love, hope, and eternal salvation.

Available Now in the Irresistible Church Series

Start with Hello
Introducing Your Church to Special Needs Ministry

Families with special needs often share that they desire two things in their church: accessibility and acceptance. Accessibility to existing structures, programs and people is an imperative. Acceptance with a sense of belonging by the others who also participate in the structures, programs and fellowship of the church is equally necessary. In this simple book you'll learn the five steps to becoming an accessible and accepting church.

To receive first notice of upcoming resources, including respite, inclusive worship and support groups, please contact us at churchrelations@joniandfriends.org.

Other Recommended Resources

Beyond Suffering Bible

The *Beyond Suffering Bible* by Joni and Friends is the first study Bible made specifically for those who suffer and the people who love them. Uplifting insights from Joni Eareckson Tada and numerous experts and scholars who have experienced suffering in their own lives and will help you move beyond the "why" of suffering to grasp the eternal value God is building into our lives. Special features include: inspiring devotionals, biblical and contemporary profiles, Bible reading plans, connection points and disability ministry resources.

Find out more at http://www.joniandfriends.org/store/category/bibles/

Beyond Suffering® *Student Edition*

Beyond Suffering for the Next Generation: A Christian View on Disability Ministry will equip young people to consider the issues that affect people with disabilities and their families, and inspire them to action. Students who embrace this study will gain confidence to join a growing, worldwide movement that God is orchestrating to fulfill Luke 14:21-23: "Go out quickly into the streets and alleys of the town and bring in the poor, the crippled, the blind, and the lame.... so that my house will be full."

ISBN: 978-0-9838484-6-2
304 pages · 8.5" x 11"
Includes CD-ROM

Joni: *An Unforgettable Story*

In this unforgettable autobiography, Joni reveals each step of her struggle to accept her disability and discover the meaning of her life. The hard-earned truths she discovers and the special ways God reveals his love are testimonies to faith's triumph over hardship and suffering. This new edition includes an afterword, in which Joni talks about the events that have occurred in her life since the book's original publication in 1976, including her marriage and the expansion of her worldwide ministry to families affected by disability.

ISBN: 978-0310240013
205 pages · Paperback

Customizable Resources from the Book

Available for Download at
http://www.joniandfriends.org/church-relations/

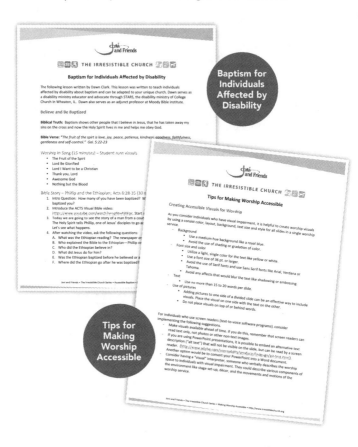

Baptism for Individuals Affected by Disability

Tips for Making Worship Accessible